Contents

What is a frog?

A frog is an **amphibian**. It spends part of its life living in water, and part of its life on land.

Amphibians lay their eggs in water. They live in wet places, often near ponds or lakes.

⇦ Common frogs have smooth, damp skin and golden eyes.

Some frogs live in wet **rainforests**. They are called tree frogs. Most tree frogs are much smaller than frogs that live on the ground.

⇨ This tree frog's big red eyes and orange feet scare other animals away.

Eye

Foot

The story of a frog

A young frog is called a **tadpole**. It looks quite different from a frog!

This small animal begins its life as an egg. The amazing story of how it becomes an adult frog is called its **life cycle**.

1

Egg

6

2

Tadpole

⇐A frog goes
through three
stages in its life
cycle. It spends all
of the first two
stages in water.

3

Frog

Frogspawn

In spring, male and female frogs come together to **mate**. They always mate in water.

A male grasps a female tightly. As the female lays her eggs, the male covers them with a liquid. The liquid **fertilizes** the eggs.

Only fertilized eggs grow into tadpoles. The eggs are as soft as jelly. They stick together in a big clump called **frogspawn**.

⇩The frogspawn swells and floats to the surface of the water.

9

Inside the eggs

Once the eggs are laid, the adult frogs swim away. Inside each egg, a new tadpole is growing.

The tadpole feeds on a small **yolk** in the egg, and grows bigger.

⇨A female frog may lay hundreds of eggs at a time.

Many of the eggs are eaten by fish and other pond animals. But some survive, and their tadpoles keep growing.

After a few weeks, the eggs hatch. They hatch sooner in warm weather than they do in cold weather.

11

Tiny tadpoles

Tadpoles are tiny when they hatch, but they quickly grow.

Each tadpole has a long tail, which it uses to swim. It has feathery **gills** on either side of its head. These allow the young tadpole to breathe underwater.

To begin with, tadpoles just eat small, green water plants. Later, they will also eat pond animals, such as water fleas.

⇨Tadpoles feed and grow. They grow faster when they live in warm water with plenty of food.

Tail

Gills

The big change

When they are about seven weeks old, tadpoles begin to change into frogs.

First, they grow back legs. A few weeks later, their gills disappear. Then they swim to the surface of the water to breathe air.

⇧ As its legs grow longer, the tail grows shorter.

⇦ Then its front legs begin to grow.

⇦ The tadpole's back legs grow first.

Their tails begin to shrink and their front legs begin to grow. The tadpoles now look like tiny frogs.

⇩By the time it is 12 weeks old, the tiny frog is about 3 centimetres long.

4

15

Froglets

The little frogs keep growing, and their tails disappear. They are now called froglets.

The froglets stay in, or near, water. They feed on small **insects**, which they catch with their long, sticky tongues.

⇨ Froglets can swim, crawl, hop, and climb onto the floating leaves of lilies.

When they are bigger, the froglets move away from their pond.

They find a safe place under some plants, where they can hide.

⇨ This froglet is hiding in a pitcher plant in a wood.

The life of a frog

Adult frogs spend most of their time on land. They hide from animals that hunt them for food.

Frogs rest during the day. In the evening they hunt for insects, slugs and worms.

18

⇩Frogs can make huge leaps to catch food with their long tongues.

Tongue

⇩Camouflage helps a frog to hide from animals that want to eat it.

Many frogs have green, grey or brown skin. They blend in with their surroundings and so are hard to see. This is called **camouflage**.

Back to the pond

Frogs **hibernate** in winter.
This is because there is
little food to eat, and
the weather is cold.

When animals hibernate,
they fall into a deep
sleep to save energy.

⇧ Frogs hibernate under
rocks, in burrows or
in ponds.

In spring, frogs return to the pond where they were born. This is where the adult frogs mate. Soon the story of the life cycle will begin again.

⇧Male tree frogs croak loudly to call the female to mate.

⇩Frogs are ready to mate when they are two to three years old.

21

Glossary

Amphibian
An animal that spends the first part of its life cycle in water, and the second part mostly on land.

Camouflage
Patterns and colours that help an animal to hide.

Fertilize
When liquid from a male changes female eggs so that they can grow into new living things.

Frogspawn
A clump of frog's eggs.

Gills
The parts of a tadpole's body that allow it to breathe underwater.

Hibernate
To spend the cold winter months in a kind of deep sleep.

Insect
A small animal with six legs. A water flea is a type of insect.

Life cycle
The story of how a living thing changes from birth to death and how it has young.

Mate
When a male and female animal come together to produce new life.

Rainforest
A forest that has a lot of rain all year round.

Tadpole
When a young frog hatches from its egg and lives all the time in water.

Yolk
The part of an egg that feeds the growing tadpole.

Index

Notes for parents and teachers

- Look through the book and talk about the pictures.

- Safety outdoors. Teach children how to stay safe while investigating animals and their life cycles, especially when they are around water.

- Respect for wildlife. Teach children how to observe and, if appropriate, handle animals with care. They should observe animals in their natural environment, without disturbing wildlife and their habitats. Frogspawn should not be moved from one pond to another, as this allows viruses and other diseases to spread.

- Frog activities. Draw the life cycle of a frog and label the different stages together. Use the Internet to research poison arrow frogs, and find out how they defend themselves.

- Visit a wildlife garden or park together and learn about pond habitats. Talk about the ways that a habitat provides an animal with the food and shelter it needs to survive. Find out which other animals live in a pond habitat.

- Be prepared for questions about human life cycles. Talking about a child's family helps them to link life processes, such as reproduction, to their own experience. Drawing simple family trees and looking at photo albums are fun ways to engage young children.